Mental Health

The Inclusive Church Resource

DARTON · LONGMAN + TODD

First published in Great Britain in 2014 by
Darton, Longman and Todd Ltd
1 Spencer Court
140 – 142 Wandsworth High Street
London SW18 4JJ

Reprinted 2016, 2018

ISBN 978-0-232-53066-7

A catalogue record for this book is available from the
British Library

Phototypeset by Judy Linard
Printed and bound in Great Britain by
Bell & Bain Ltd, Glasgow.

Contents

Acknowledgements

Inclusive Church is grateful to all who have made this book possible.

In particular we would like to acknowledge the enthusiasm and support for this book from David Moloney at Darton, Longman and Todd.

This book arose from conferences that St Martin-in-the-Fields and Inclusive Church ran together. The insights from these conferences were the springboard for this book.

We are grateful to the Churches Equality Practitioner Group for ideas and suggestions for this book series.

We would especially like to thank those who have generously given of their time and contributed stories, reflections and resources for this book.

It is our hope that all that is shared here will encourage others to go further in the work of creating a more inclusive and welcoming church.

About Inclusive Church

Inclusive Church was formed in 2003. From the start, churches and individuals have signed up to the statement of belief as a way of indicating their desire to see a more accepting and open church.

The Inclusive Church
'Statement of Belief'

We believe in inclusive church – church which does not discriminate, on any level, on grounds of economic power, gender, mental health, physical ability, race or sexuality. We believe in church which welcomes and serves all people in the name of Jesus Christ; which is scripturally faithful; which seeks to proclaim the Gospel afresh for each generation; and which, in the power of the Holy Spirit, allows all people to grasp how wide and long and high and deep is the love of Jesus Christ.
www.inclusive-church.org.uk

Introduction
EVA MCINTYRE

*The Revd Eva McIntyre is Co-ordinator
of Mental Health Matters, a project of the
Committee for Ministry with and among
Deaf and Disabled People, and part of the
Archbishops' Council of the Church
of England. Eva is also the author of*
A Quiet Mind: Uniting body, mind and
emotions in Christian spirituality.
(Circle Books, 2011).

It is a great privilege to be writing the
Introduction to this important book. As the Co-
ordinator of the Church of England's project
Mental Health Matters I am indebted to
Inclusive Church for the incredible support and
co-working that has made it possible to raise the
profile of mental health work. The partnership
has grown and the work we do together has
blossomed. This book is one of the ways in
which that work has taken on a new life and
I am excited that such a useful and accessible
resource is going to be available to our churches.

When I first began to explore the

subject of mental health at a national level, it was as though I'd opened a floodgate. The communication I received came predominantly from two areas; first, those living with mental illness and those caring for them, who were struggling to stay within the church, and second, those in the church who felt 'isolated at the coal face' as they looked for resources with a faith perspective and for support with what they had come to realise was a challenging ministry.

As the last four years have passed, the flood of interest and enquiries has not dried up, if anything it has increased. At the Greenbelt Festival over the last two years, we have been staggered at the interest and need, as the queue of people at the Inclusive Church stall has been constant and long; made up of people with lived experience, carers, health care professionals, teachers and lecturers, clergy and lay workers, all wanting to know what support and resources we can supply to help them in their ministry.

The statistics tell us that one in four people will experience mental illness in their lifetime. This figure is based on those who go to their GP and receive a diagnosis; the real figure is likely to be much higher. Mental illness is no respecter of age, gender, race, class or education. None of us is immune; at the drop of a hat, our lives can change and bring us to a point of crisis and then we are one of those 'statistics', whether we go to the GP for help or suffer in silence, afraid of the stigma that will attach to us if we acknowledge what is happening.

When I first spoke out about my past experience of depression and anxiety, I wasn't sure what the response would be. As I stood at the church door, one after another, people confided in me, 'I'm one of four, too!', and so we were no longer alone. It's as simple as that to begin the journey towards mutual support and trust. I remember, too, the look of incredulity on the face of a woman in the prison where I was chaplain a few years ago. She was feeling very low and I'd shared some of the techniques I'd learned to help me cope on bad days. 'You? You can't ever feel like this!' – it was more of a question than a statement of fact – 'But you're so strong!' It was strange that, simply in admitting my own weakness, I had given her something to grab hold of and help her stay afloat in the turbulent waters of her emotions. Later, she expressed a sense of vocation: I had no doubt that, if she did follow the path of a vocation to ordination, she would make a fine priest. God calls us not in spite of our struggles with our mental health but because of them.

A few years ago, an unwelcome caller came to the vicarage and stayed to harass me for months. The members of my congregations who had dared to share their own stories with me in the past, watched as I unravelled through fear, stress and lack of sleep. I was now more than someone who had experienced mental illness in the past; I became a living, breathing parable. Over the weeks, every member of my two churches who had ever experienced depression, anxiety or any other kind of mental illness, gravitated towards me. They stood next to me and chose the words with which to say, 'I know something of what you're going through'. It was an immense comfort to have their solidarity.

In these dark weeks, I found solace in a phrase from St Paul, 'In my weakness, I am strong' (2 Cor. 12:10), and one night, as I lay awake in terror, I placed the Bible open at this page on the pillow next to me. I've often struggled with St Paul's writings, but in those few words I knew that he too had been to this dark place. My relationship with his writing was changed in that moment. I was profoundly grateful that throughout this experience I could feel the presence of God and that my spiritual life was richly deepened. This is so often not the case when you are living with depression or anxiety, and those who feel abandoned and out of God's reach experience a double suffering. My mind inevitably recites the words of Psalm 22, quoted by Jesus on the cross, 'My God, my God, why have you forsaken me?' Yet, time and again, I hear people say that, if they had their time again, they would not avoid the experience of depression because it made them a more complete and compassionate person. I have heard similar things said by some who live with more severe and long-term mental health conditions, but we must be careful not to assume that everyone sees their illness as a gift or a blessing; for many it is a constant struggle and a life-limiting condition. All too often, mental illness leads to stigma, isolation and poverty.

Engagement with people living with mental illness has been shown to be one of the most important and challenging areas of work for the churches to be involved with; when we say 'one in four' we're not talking about anonymous statistics but members of our own congregations and clergy, our families and neighbours, our friends and colleagues. Yet mental health work in the church is given a pitifully low profile and priority at a national or regional level. As funding for NHS work diminishes, the need for constructive support in the local community grows, but there is so little provision and mental health charities are stretched to breaking point. Just think: even at the level of that conservative 'one in four' statistic, with a UK population of 63,000,000 that's 15,750,000 people. The church has a history of pioneering in health and social care and I believe it is time for us to step up to the challenge of working in the area of mental health.

The good news is that research undertaken by the Time to Change campaign has found that faith communities, for the most part, do an excellent job of welcoming and supporting people with mental illness. I have seen first-hand evidence of this as I've visited projects – simple and extensive – run by local churches. From 'knit and natter groups' and café drop-ins, to mental health forums and training initiatives. In Romsey, the Triangulate project that educates employers about the mental health needs of their staff was born in the abbey congregation and is impacting far outside it. In Liverpool, a pioneering project has been set up, to bring together people with mental health issues in safe and supportive church environments throughout the city. This is to name but a few of the inspiring projects and initiatives. The church can be good news to those with mental illness. And in Essex, they've gone beyond the boundaries of the church to set up Essex Mind and Spirit, a multi-faith network that demonstrates working together at its best. There is much to celebrate, but there is also so much more to be done. As churches, to undertake this work, we need to be equipped and educated on the subject of mental health, not only practically and professionally but also on the theological, historical and pastoral imperatives for doing this work.

In 2012 a headline in a Sunday tabloid caused a stir: 'Jesus Christ may have struggled with mental illness, says the Church of England'. It was, of course, a sub-editor's act of cunning and mischief. It didn't accurately reflect the content of the article, which was quoting from a sermon suggestion I'd provided on the internet. In this sermon, I'd referred to the fact that Jesus was not immune to the accusation that he was mentally ill and cited the Bible passage which clearly describes the arrival of Jesus' mother, sisters and brothers who want to take him home because they think he has 'lost his mind'. The reaction, which went global, was fascinating. I was even branded a heretic and apostate for daring to suggest that Jesus would have been so flawed! To some, Jesus being *perfect* means that he is *flawless*, but in my understanding it means that he is *complete*. I could cite verses that show how Jesus suffered such anguish that I am sure he would be able to identify with our deepest mental and emotional suffering, but it's not necessary here because the authors have provided all that is necessary.

In the pages of this book you will find the theological expertise of John Swinton and the pastoral insight of Jean Vanier – all that you will need to make the case for mental health being a top priority for your church and, indeed, all churches in the UK. You will also read real-life accounts – those from the experience of the authors of the Theology section of the book and those of the four contributors who have told their personal stories in the Experience section. For some, these stories will resonate with personal experience, for others they will be a source of enlightenment. For all of us, they will touch our hearts and tenderise us for this work, which is a profound privilege as well as an essential ministry.

PART 1
Experience

*Stories from lived experience are central
to this book. It would be easy to skip
this section and read the theological
reflection or look at the resources. The
stories here are real and speak of what it
is like to live with mental health issues
in different forms. We are grateful to
these storytellers for their honesty. Our
theological reflection and practical
outworking should follow from
these accounts of lived experience,
so please take time to read these
stories carefully.*

Paul's story

*Paul Taylor is married to Jo, who is a deputy
ward manager. They have three children
and a golden retriever. Before ordination
Paul worked as a nurse in the operating
department. He loves non-league football.
Since retirement on medical grounds he
works part-time as a hospital chaplain.*

Sitting in the corner of my study one Monday morning, crying for no reason, I knew something was wrong, just not what.

But a lot had happened before I got to this point. My name is Paul, I trained as a nurse, working in acute medicine, and then in the operating theatre. This took me from Preston to London to Derby. I am a priest in the Church of England, though not working for the Church of England. That will make sense, I promise. I am married to Jo who is a nurse. We have three children, and our golden retriever.

We can all find ourselves fitting into some type of descriptive box, or being a statistic. It took me nearly 30 years to discover mine.

Let's look at some of the boxes and statistics

that I find myself in, that contribute to making up this person 'Paul':

- 1 in 4 people in the UK will experience a mental health problem each year. **Tick.**
- 9 out of 10 people with mental health problems experience stigma and discrimination. **Tick.**
- Bipolar disorder is relatively common. Around 1 person in 100 is diagnosed with the condition. **Tick.**
- Bipolar disorder can occur at any age, although it often develops between the ages of 18 and 24 years. Men and women from all backgrounds are equally likely to develop bipolar disorder. **Tick.**
- Coupled with the increase of stress and related illness in clergy, and clergy burnout. **Tick.**

As I sat in that corner, I did not realise I was joining a new group. Thankfully my GP was able to see me straight away, and signed me off with stress and depression. I had to make a hard call to my line manager.

A couple of months prior to this I had been off with a broken foot, while playing football for the local side in a fun match. That was no problem. Stress however was frightening, the fear that I would be seen as weak and a failure.

I could look back to another time of high stress, as a newly qualified staff nurse. I struggled, like a duck floating on the pond, with legs paddling like mad underneath. I felt isolated, not wanting to go to work. I had a great sense of panic, wanting to run away. This feeling had to end, so I took an overdose and ended up in A&E. I knew the treatment would not be sympathetic, with your stomach pumped almost as a punishment; then a brief chat with the psychiatrist the following day. I knew the answers to give, which meant that it was back to work as if nothing had happened. It is so different to how it is today. In those days there was no occupational health counselling. It was friends and a colleague who helped me through.

Moving forward to my 40s finds me as vicar of two rural parishes, which sounds great. We lived in a lovely vicarage. Trying to bring about change was not easy, and more than once I found myself in situations that could be described as being bullied. There were examples of little things to undermine, maybe a sly word or comment. Or there were more obvious examples, with letters of complaint, abusive telephone calls, constant criticism over any new initiative. Here in the institution of the church, I was being bullied – it was a shock. It took its toll, and I had my first breakdown.

My GP asked if I could be moved to a quiet country parish for a rest. I explained I was already in a rural parish, known in church circles as Dibley! On returning to work I was lucky to have a member of the clergy as a mentor. A retired clergyman, he was there as my support, and had vast experience. I had his phone number by my desk, 'the hotline' he called it. He gave me the confidence to carry on.

Life was a struggle, and we ended up moving parishes after five years. In the new church I worked in a team, and things were good. However, I had not taken into account the impact that the previous five years had taken on my health, living under almost constant stress. I had what some would describe as a breakdown. For me it was complete physical and mental collapse. I had been in hospital for a few days with a migraine; Jo came to bring me home. As we approached the vicarage, I had a choking sensation, and fear and panic. I physically could not enter the house. My head had racing thoughts that I could not stop. What followed over the next few weeks was a journey to a place I never want to go to again.

I had developed some very bad coping mechanisms, including self-harm. This was difficult to understand. I would cut myself on my arms using whatever I could find, not just knives, but broken plastic cups. It made no sense, except that this was something I was in control of. Trips to A&E would find my arms dressed. However, in 20 years the approach had changed to folk with mental illness. I felt I was treated no differently than when I broke my foot. Self-harm took me to a place where I could say I was ill; however, I needed to hide this shame. So it was amazing how much gardening I did that scratched my arms! At times you just want to block things out. I found myself misusing prescription drugs – I had strong painkillers and muscle relaxants for a back condition – combined with alcohol. However, Jo would lock the drink away, and then I would use the communion wine in my study. Things came to a head when the children went away for half-term. I agreed to spend three days in the psychiatric unit – which was like being on retreat.

I received good care from a priest who had worked in mental health as a chaplain. I was told that while I was off sick, I could not attend church within the team. My children attended various church groups, so my wife would take them, and I would have to find somewhere else. The congregation had been told they could not make contact. I had been, and was, their pastor, and had journeyed with some of them through their difficult times. They wanted to care for us as a family, but were being denied. It felt like I was suddenly the outcast from this community. I would hide if I saw someone when I was walking the dog. Walking around Tesco, I nearly fell into the freezer as a member of the congregation came up the aisle.

To move forward, we had a formal visit from the church leadership with a message. The bishop would like me to go on 'gardening leave' (I had not heard the term before, and we had only a small garden!), then to take early retirement due to ill health. I was just 45 years old.

At this stage it was hard to take in, for I was still not well. After five years of training, and working in various parishes, this was it, the end. I really felt not wanted, an embarrassment to the church. Then things hit me. Where will we live? How will we manage? Depression was to hit again. There was a move backwards for a while, and some old coping mechanisms reappeared. Try explaining to health care professionals how the church works! There are no human resources personnel for clergy. We were under pressure to move out of the vicarage, bringing more stress and more pressure. We had identified stress as one of the triggers to my depression.

All I could see was everything ending; I could not see the future. My registration as a nurse had expired years ago. I felt that decisions were out of my control. It felt like I had to fight. Yes, I had a mental illness, stress and depression, although as yet I had no formal diagnosis. When I broke my foot playing football, folk in the parish accepted it, and thought it quite fun! Mental illness is quite different. I had been asked if I could guarantee I would not be ill again. Which is like asking if you will have flu again. No one knows.

In the past I had been involved in some creative projects. The church had no problem with me then, I had lots of creative energy. Looking back I realise that these and other situations have been while I was in a manic state. It was 18 months after I retired that the diagnosis of bipolar disorder was made.

In preparation for retirement I drew together my farewell service; it was the saddest liturgy I had ever compiled. We moved into a new property rented from the church. I struggled to find purpose; I had lost my identity in the community and my sense of vocation. Practical issues became a concern, for example, what to do with my time? My wife went to work, the children were at sixth form and school, which left me on my own. I found myself asking if this was it, was this my life? I looked for opportunities to fill my time and found the voluntary sector very welcoming. I was open about my illness from the start, so that folk would understand. I worked in a charity shop for half a day each week. I attended an art therapy group, and volunteered half a day with the hospital chaplaincy. On retiring I wanted to have permission from the bishop to help in the church we attended. When it came, it was very restrictive, with conversations between the vicar of the church where we worshipped and the hospital chaplaincy. The decision was made, but without contact with my health care professionals for their input.

As someone with a mental health illness, you get the feeling that somehow you are more difficult to deal with within the institution of the 'church'. Christians with depression need an atmosphere of acceptance to deal healthily with mental health issues.

This is just a brief whistle-stop tour of my story, which I hope gives you a flavour of the journey. In a naive way I believed the church would be open to all. However, my experience makes me feel that I am on the outside of the institution and an embarrassment.

When I retired, I was encouraged that by moving from the stress of a parish I could develop a new and creative ministry within the diocese. I did not really grasp that at the time. It has taken me five years to make sense of it. I enjoyed parish ministry, and having it removed from me hurt deeply. I truly believed that was what I was called to do.

I have recently moved to a new post, two and a half days a week as Anglican chaplain at a local hospital. With my background in nursing and health care, as well as pastoral care, I bring something to the table. My ministry is of the interrupted journey, be that in hospital, or my work as a safety steward at a football club, or within the Red Cross. This is my new and creative ministry, free from the stress of a parish.

So why as a priest in the C of E do I still feel an outcast because I suffer with a mental illness?

Liz's story

Liz Bloomer is a member of St Michael's Church in Stourport on Severn. She is married to Brian and together they are town-centre chaplains. They share a love of folk dance and music and enjoy watching the birds who visit their garden.

I have had some severe periods of depression in the past few years and found the feelings I encountered were, to begin with, totally out of my control. I was the 'coper' in my family, the motivator in my workplace and the person who would be there to offer my services at the drop of a hat and with a smile on my face. So, finding myself unable even to look after myself properly, let alone all the other people who depended on me, left me feeling very inadequate and with little self-worth.

Depression is a very emotive subject for me, especially among people who have never had to live with it. It is that hidden disability that no one really understands fully – least of all those who suffer with it. The symptoms include feeling overwhelmingly tired, angry, emotional and with a need to withdraw from the world around you. In my case I felt that I should be able to solve all of the problems around me, but then felt extreme guilt and failure at not being able to do so. This can go on for many weeks or months and sometimes years without some form of treatment. Seeking treatment can also make you feel even more depressed as you feel that you are even more of a failure at not being able to get through it on your own. The most important thing I have learned is that people with depression need to be able to recognise and accept what is happening before anything can move on, and some never do.

I held a busy post as an inclusion officer, heavily involved in disability discrimination and the rights and needs of children with special needs and disabilities and their families. My role was to support the inclusion of children into provision alongside their able-bodied peers, supporting families and providers of early years education and childcare. My daughter was born with no problems initially, apart from being a little premature, but 'failed to thrive', as the doctors put it. However, as time went by, she had many delays in her development. She was diagnosed with mild to moderate learning disabilities and had a Statement of Special Educational needs by the age of eight. My interest in this area of children's lives took off from there.

My battles with health and education throughout her life resulted in me studying the subject at university and gaining a degree at the age of 47. I got the job of inclusion officer before the results were published and felt so proud. Here I was with all the research in front of me and I was going to change so much for children in the future! Not quite! I found myself once again in the minority, fighting my cause and losing out for the people I cared so passionately about when my funding was redirected to other more 'important' areas. I continued to fight on, both for my daughter and at work.

Crunch time came when an additional family problem made my world come crashing down. All I could remember thinking was how everyone carried on with what, at that time, I thought were silly and senseless things when my world was fraught with pain and worry. I was not sleeping and felt so tired all the time. My relationships with everyone were deteriorating rapidly. This included my relationship with my husband. I became desperate and angry with myself for not coping. Then one day, a colleague put her arms around me and held me tight and suggested that I should see a doctor. I cried then and continued to cry for weeks afterwards. In fact crying and sleeping made up most of my days. I had completely stopped leaving the house and couldn't even cope with too many visitors. With the help of a community psychiatric nurse, I slowly began to rebuild my life, looking back at the factors which had led me to this breakdown.

After a few weeks my husband suggested to me that I return to church. I have always had a strong faith, but even that had deserted me in the preceding weeks. I was unsure of how I would be received and did not want to fall apart in front of everyone. I knew that if anyone uttered any kind words towards me I would just howl with tears and then feel guilty for ruining their day. Also I was afraid that if anyone asked me to do anything, I would not be able to stop myself from saying yes and therefore take on even more pressure. I am a people-pleaser. Nothing is more important to me than ensuring everyone else is happy. When I do say no, the guilt I feel then worries me for days to come and makes me think I should have said yes in the first instance.

Encounters with friends and family also had an impact on my daily life. As a smiley person who wants everyone to feel welcomed and special, I found it so difficult to even give eye contact; let alone go out of the house for long enough to actually meet people. Comments like 'pull yourself together' and 'stop being so negative' and 'what's up with you today?' all pointed to the fact that others definitely see the problem as your fault and nothing at all to do with them.

There is no doubt that some of the fault was mine. I had let myself, and my body's resources, run dry and had nothing left to give. Instead of taking time out to refresh my body and soul I'd continued to try and give, and of course could not. I couldn't help it because it always seemed so selfish to me to concentrate on myself rather than others.

It took all my energy and a helping hand from my husband to go back to church. Some members of the congregation were most supportive, but others just did not understand. I spent a lot of my time in deep thought, which could well have seemed to others as being unfriendly; as turning on my usual smile was very difficult to do. Those members of the church who understood would often visit me and we would sit together in the sunshine, listening to the birdsong and quietly letting nature take its course. Being outside in this wonderful world that God had created was very inspirational to me. When telling work colleagues that the only thing I felt I must do each day was feed the birds, I remember one of them telling me to 'get a life'. They had little idea that those very birds had given me part of my life back! Many church members and work colleagues stayed away from me. Some people could deal with the tears and others would be embarrassed. Would this have been so if I had broken my leg? I do doubt it.

This I found to be most distressing as I consider church to be the one place where everyone should be welcome and I believe that fellowship, care and support is fundamental to church life. A welcoming ear or a warm hug are sometimes all you need to carry on to the next day, but to be ignored or dismissed can set you back for weeks when you're struggling with depression.

The visits to church became easier and I found that I gained so much, particularly from the services using the Celtic spirituality of Iona. The simplicity and natural resources got through to me in a way that other worship did not. The silence and reflection were a way of nurturing my soul and taking time to listen to God. While some of the triggers to my depression were still in my mind, I was able to find ways of dealing with them and placing the negative aspects of my life into God's hands.

These triggers will, I suppose, always be with me: the need to help and care for others, to solve all of their problems, to be the one who takes others' problems on board knowing that I probably cannot do a great deal to solve the situations.

A very memorable Celtic service had a huge impact on me being able to let go. It was autumn and on entering church, I found a large brown but beautifully formed horse chestnut leaf on my seat. They were scattered around the church. The service centred on the fall of leaves from the trees to make room for the waiting buds to burst open in the spring. The tree needed to give up its leaves to encourage new life, just as I had to relinquish my worries into God's hands for my life to move on. I had to put my trust in him. I walked around the church firmly clutching my leaf, not wanting to let it go into the waiting basket but knowing that this is what I needed to do. As the leaf left my hands, I can only remember hearing the howl of emotion which left my body and feeling the tears run down my cheeks. I was supported by many of the church members, but the feeling I most remember is the feeling of freedom, a fresh start and hope for the future. As I write these words, those feelings surge through me again and I think will be there for ever more.

I became stronger and happier. I was able to reduce the levels of medication which had been prescribed and I had taken more time out to make decisions about the capacity I had to help others. Although I still felt a little uncomfortable about putting myself at the centre of my life, I had come to realise that unless I could nurture and love myself, I would never be able to give help to anyone else. My determination to lead a much simpler and less stressful life was a priority to me now. After six months, I was able to deal with everyday events and began to take on some of the more meaningful things in my life. However, the nature of my character makes me more prone to suffering with depression. I have to work hard not to take on too much. When I do, I can feel myself sliding back and know that I have to take action. The difference now is that I can recognise those times, feel better equipped to deal with them and do not slide back as far as I have in the past.

I am still a people-pleaser and often feel that I ought to be helping others more than is practicable. Of course, people still ask me to take on all sorts of tasks, even though they know about my depression – but to them, I suppose, I look 'better' ... and as a people-pleaser it is still difficult to say no.

My faith is more important to me than ever. I know that God has never thought me to be weak or a failure. His unconditional love for me shines through and my hope is that now I may act as a light to others who, through reading this, may see a way to cope with the illness that is depression. The recovery from depression is a long one. It cannot be rushed and often takes the form of three steps forward and two back. I now realise that this is healthy. I used to think that depression had taken away six months of my life but now realise that it gave me the time to reflect on who I am and the time to learn to love myself: depression has, ironically, *given* me life.

Miriam's story

Miriam Hodson was diagnosed with bipolar affective disorder in 1996 at the age of 29. She now works as a mental health consultant, which includes training, public speaking, writing and organising conferences. She is also a trained and experienced play therapist.

This is the story of some of my experiences of living with the diagnosis of bipolar affective disorder, the ways I feel churches sometimes react to this, how they can improve things for people like me, and how important my faith has been in my journey towards healing.

Before my first admission to a psychiatric unit in 1996 at the age of 29, I was very career orientated and had no noticeable symptoms of mental health problems. After an incredibly stressful year I had my first breakdown, though to me it felt more of a 'breakup', of life as I knew it. I was totally devastated when I wasn't well enough to go back to my job. It seemed like my life was over. It felt like a total loss of everything. Financial security, friends, routine, confidence and most importantly hope. I also felt like everyone could tell.

After several manic episodes, severe depressions and hospital admissions I was diagnosed with bipolar affective disorder, or manic depression, as many call it. This causes people to experience periods of very extreme moods, both highs and lows.

At this stage I felt totally stuck in the mental health system. I thought that the only other people who could understand me were those who had been through similar experiences and professionals who were trained to 'deal' with us. I spent years sitting in drop-ins and day centres, believing that life could never have meaning and purpose again. I was also scared of the stigma I felt I was likely to face if I went out into the big wide world. It felt like psychiatrists had given me a lifelong label and written me off.

I was then very fortunate to come across the recovery movement. The recovery movement works towards changing attitudes within the psychiatric system and in wider society. They believe you can move beyond the label; that you can recover, or learn to live with, and cope with, symptoms – that you can move on and lead a fulfilling life. I personally prefer the term 'healing' to 'recovery'. Recovery makes it sound like you are going back to where you were before, whereas for me it is about moving forward to become more whole. The recovery movement gave me hope and confidence. I am most proud of qualifying and working as a mental health trainer. I also slowly began to believe friends could understand more than I gave them credit for. My friends are now one of the most important sources of support and joy in my life.

I was brought up in a devout Baptist family, so I don't remember a time when God wasn't in my life. As I became a teenager I started to feel that the God I had grown up with was really judgemental and that a lot of things I was starting to believe in were sinful. This caused huge conflict and confusion. After my mental health diagnosis I was an occasional churchgoer, though I never really found a church that I felt understood me and where I could belong. Although I still had my faith, I felt very angry with God for what I was going through. I then met a very wise nun who told me that God really didn't mind me being angry with him and that he more than anyone else understood the reasons why. It is one of the most helpful things anyone has ever said to me.

I still need to go into hospital sometimes. When I get manic, I can't stop talking, can't stay in one place and have very strange delusions. One of the most extreme examples is when I believed I was the modern-day John the Baptist, come to prepare the way for my sister's unborn baby, who was going to be the returning messiah. Even when she was born a girl I was delighted that Jesus had chosen to come back as a woman.

I have also had some really beautiful experiences and visions – like seeing angels, and sitting on top of a hill in Lancashire for four hours, totally believing I was in heaven. I once went to a service at Sheffield Cathedral. The only other people there were three women sitting on the other side of the chapel. A sunbeam suddenly shone down on them, through the beautiful stained-glass window, and I had an overwhelming feeling that they were God the mother, God the daughter and God the Holy Spirit. A psychiatrist would probably call this a delusion or a hallucination, but to me it felt much more like a metaphor and still feels very special and real. A gift from God. There is a fine line between mystical and psychotic experiences. I think that probably a lot of the saints and prophets of old would nowadays end up in the psychiatric system.

A lot of people have really terrible and frightening experiences. I did for example believe I was in hell once, walking lost through Hackney on a freezing February night. I feel it is probably through my faith that most of my experiences have been of a positive and often beautiful nature.

When I am low I just feel I am in a big void. I have heard people say they meet God in their dark places, but I feel like I am completely on my own. I don't necessarily stop believing in God, though sometimes that is the case. I just feel like he is behind a big black cloud. I do, however, believe that my faith has helped me stay alive when I have felt suicidal. When I am totally depressed I am unable to read, but as I start to feel better I find huge comfort in reading the Bible, particularly the psalms. I also read Job and take great strength from the way he dealt with his horrific experiences. I also read the Passion, which reminds me of how Christ more than anyone understands my suffering. For me the only positive things about depression are that when I come out the other end, it makes me appreciate good times more and that it gives me more empathy when others are having a hard time.

I feel very fortunate that about five years ago, a friend told me about Inclusive Church. I first arrived at one gathering, very upset on a cold and wet Sunday evening. I cried the whole way through the service and was very surprised that it felt very comforting and okay. I love the church by candlelight and the simplicity and peaceful atmosphere of the Sunday evening services. I love the regularity of the liturgy, though also the way our church explores new ways of doing things. I love the music – both singing and listening to the choir. I also enjoy the inspirational and often thought-provoking sermons. I started to believe this church really was striving to be an inclusive and that the church could finally provide somewhere I could truly belong and that God would accept me just as I am.

I slowly got to know the congregation and I generally found people friendly and non-judgemental. People were asking how I was, out of general interest, not watching to see if I was high or low, like professionals do or unfortunately at times my friends too. I felt I was blending in and feeling like a normal person – whatever that is.

At other times this is hard as you do want people to understand and be able to support you when unwell. I did slowly start telling people and was amazed so many people had also had similar experiences. We started to support each other and several of them have become very close friends.

I do sometimes feel excluded. Some people don't understand and get annoyed when I have to get up and walk around in services due to mania and side-effects of medication. I am very lucky at my church that the staff are very understanding. I have heard of churches where people have been asked to leave or even barred from church for a while. If somebody does become too disruptive to stay in church, it would really help if someone could go outside and talk to them, try to understand and let them know that they are still valued, as part of the congregation. Ongoing support then needs to be provided. It worries me that clergy and other members of pastoral teams very rarely have training about the symptoms of mental health problems and how to work with people who are extremely distressed. I think it would also help to have dedicated people in the church who know about mental health.

When I am manic I talk incredibly fast and sometimes don't make sense. Please try to listen to me and don't just walk away. Sometimes there is a lot of sense in what I am saying if you take the time to listen, and even if there isn't you can normally tell what emotions I am feeling and feedback to me how I seem. Sometimes, when I am psychotic, I may tell you completely mad things, like some of the stories I have talked about above. Again you can listen and try to put yourself in the situation of understanding what it feels like to be in the world I am experiencing. If you bluntly tell me you don't believe what I am saying, rather than understanding it is my reality, you will upset me or make me angry.

One of the most hurtful things that can happen when I am manic is that people walk away because they don't know what to say or do. I believe that one of the biggest causes of exclusion is fear. People are scared they will make things worse. It is okay to say you don't know what to say or do. We are all individuals and have different needs, so just ask how you can help.

Unfortunately I think there are also theological reasons that people are scared of mental illness. In biblical times the only framework of understanding was in terms of demon possession. Although most people have moved beyond this now, there are still churches that perform exorcisms, so there are obviously people who still in some way believe this is true. If a person themselves believes they are possessed by demons it can be helpful to go through this process, but I have heard of people almost being forced into it and not having the psychological elements of their problems recognised. This is so damaging.

I have also had people saying to me that if my faith was strong enough God would take away my mental health problems. At times when I am particularly vulnerable, this is incredibly upsetting. It just adds guilt to all the other difficult feelings I experience.

I also find people don't know what to say when I come out of a psychiatric ward, in a way they would when someone has a physical problem. One simple thing is that people just don't seem to think about sending get-well cards or flowers.

I feel that sometimes when I volunteer to do things within the church, my offers aren't taken up. I worry that this is because it is considered I may be unreliable or display extreme behaviour.

When I am depressed I find it very hard to get myself to church. In a big church it sometimes feels like people don't notice when you can't make it. It really helps lift my spirits if people make the effort to contact me, to tell me I am missed. Sometimes it can make it much easier to go, if someone arranges to meet me first.

I find healing services very powerful and I have come more and more to value the power of prayer and the comfort I feel when I know people are praying for me. When you don't know what to do or say, the one thing you can do is pray and let the person you are praying for know you are. It is a true expression of compassion and Christian love.

Mary's story

Mary is a Cornish lassie with a somewhat Welsh-sounding name – Mary Jones – but it used to be Jago. Having lived in Cornwall all her life, and married with one son, she loves cliff walks, cats, gardening, friends and family, and practises mindfulness, which helps when the low times come back.

Hello and welcome to a snapshot of me, my life, and my encounter with mental illness: the swings, roundabouts and roller coasters of life, death, joy and sorrow, relationships, faith and 'the church'.

I encounter and embrace, shout and lament with and against ongoing mental dis-ease, which is a part of my life. Since a fairly recent diagnosis of Crohn's disease, I have had some extra 'down times'. I try – and don't always succeed – to practise mindfulness, compassionate meditation, and employ insights gained through therapy (more later). For the majority of my life I juggled my mental health issue, and times of complete abyss, with family life and a stressful yet somehow successful teaching

44

career – despite the stigma and discrimination. I was a music teacher and as a child music, and in particular learning to play the flute and singing, really saved me from going under in the difficulties of life then. My perfectionist streak was both a strength and a weakness, as was my stubbornness and persistence!

I now run a business in which I offer therapeutic music activity sessions for those who encounter dementia, strokes or mental illness and I work voluntarily as a spiritual and pastoral assistant in a mental health chaplaincy team, which also involves music. I take antidepressants, which I am sure enable me to feel and respond relatively 'normally' – whatever that is – to the day-to-day stresses, restrictions and rejoicings of life. Currently I am in the ordination process, hopefully towards mental health chaplaincy.

Over the past ten years I have moved in my understanding of who God is, from a wrathful, vengeance-seeking and punitive, distant and transcendent God to quite a different version. God for me now is the compassionate, non-judgemental source of all being, who was 'so chuffed with stuff she became it' through incarnation. God, who created matter, became creaturely and part of the matter of the universe, and for me now is both within and without, immanent and transcendent, metaphor and reality. God for me is a part of every micro-particle which is constantly moving, vibrating with life and in a creation-process ... and yet is still more than that. This God, for me, created and continues creating, as part of a process, a cosmos which is in constant motion towards fulfilment. A world so full of motion and change is bound to encounter collision and that for me is explanation enough of the certainty of uncertainty in life. The story of a God who rejoices with her children in their times of rejoicing and who sobs with them in the sorrows of life – all of which make us human – seems to make sense. We, as the hands and feet of that incarnate God in Jesus, run to hold the other in their times of sobbing and distress and they us. God has no other laughter that can be heard than ours as we laugh and share in the times of joy with others and them with us.

But it wasn't always this way. Far from it – except some short periods in my thirties and forties, and until more recent years. Earlier this week I was sobbing with confusion, low self-esteem, the emotional and physical pain of my ongoing Crohn's disease, the nausea of anxiety, and a heaviness of 'why me?' because I couldn't imagine those feelings (again) would pass. They always do. Sometimes it's weeks, sometimes days, sometimes even hours – depending on my resourcefulness – but they always pass. I just don't seem to remember that each time. I bet that's normal. It's still scary.

There didn't used to be any 'passing'. At around 17, this was written about me (I bravely read my psychiatric notes some years ago) after a home visit by a psychiatrist: 'We must be aware that this immature 17-year-old priest's daughter has likely inherited her mother's manic-depressive illness.' I didn't even warrant a name. I was experiencing ongoing depression and anxiety, regular stays in psychiatric hospitals, sometimes three admissions in a year (the longest was around four months, at age 18), many changes of medication to keep me up, or calm me down, plus a daily sense of foreboding and many overdose suicide attempts. It took decades for me to gain insight into these attempts, which reflected my sense of need for control over my life, my illness and indeed, control over death – of which I was terrified, but which at least offered me release from this mental pain, as did the unconsciousness and hospitalisation following each attempt. They were drastic and dangerous ways of self-harm and of getting someone to notice the agony of my mental illness and to come alongside me.

The weight of depression, the constant agitation of anxiety, and my stubborn persistence of refusal to accept that bipolar diagnosis and the ECT and drugs which would accompany it, proved exhausting, marginalising and humiliating; as did many of the mental health professional interventions I encountered – such was the culture of treatment at that time (1970s). That was a huge improvement from the era of my mother's illness, which began in the1950s – deep-sleep insulin treatment, padded cells with straitjackets, hundreds of electric convulsive therapy (ECT) treatments without anaesthetic, barbiturate drugs, a near-miss encounter with a potential frontal lobotomy and a near-fatal suicide attempt at a time when suicide was still illegal.

My mother's illness affected her personality and parenting ability – not surprising. When she was manic she was exhaustingly playful, vivacious and a spendthrift – somewhat problematical for a poverty-stricken vicar's family. When she was oscillating or descending into deep depression she became aggressive, dangerously violent and relentless in her crying which filled the house. My father was a busy, excellent priest, a man of high ideals and expectations, of patriarchal understanding regarding suitable life-roles for his daughters and who possessed, from his own Edwardian upbringing, many stereotypically judgemental beliefs concerning race, sexuality, gender and class. Appearances were all-important, so the real-life experiences of the vicarage family remained secret. Such was the nature of fear of mental health in those days, the stigma, and the exclusion by the church of those who encountered it, which was to have a tremendous impact on me when my recovery process began.

As is the case with most difficult/abusive childhoods, to me this life was the norm. I created a detailed fantasy world, in which I spent many hours at a 'number 10 Apple-Tree Lane' with 'perfect' imaginary parents who cared for small-me with an unconditional and accepting love. Later a therapist informed me my creative mind had protected and saved me from more severe mental illness and potentially total inability to cope with life. So – dream on!

My faith was an eclectic mix of Anglo-Catholicism, the *Book of Common Prayer* and Church Army Easter mission evangelism. God was omnipotent and omniscient but not much good at answering my persistent and bargaining prayers for the healing of my mother and then me. Throughout the decades, I encountered fundamentalism, evangelicalism, Brethren and Pentecostalism. They all seemed to use similar God-speak. A loving God remained elusive.

How did the change begin? I accidentally, through a personality test, fell into the hands of a psychologist, and my lengthy but worthwhile journey of therapy began. I gained insights into parent-bonding and separation/attachment issues, fear and guilt following abuse in early life, the fragility of personality and self-esteem under such conditions, which invariably led to a variety of mental health challenges and a diversity of diagnoses. The next step was a slow realisation that healing through replacing the nurturing was down to me and no one else – except perhaps an alongside, loving God. I had to begin the tortuous journey of self-discovery and self-love. It was long and arduous. Self-understanding and self-love is far from selfish but it was liberating. Additionally I needed to acquire many different techniques to manage my deep-seated default brain patterns which various stress triggers in life could – and still can – bring into play and take me down old familiar routes of depression, reduced self-esteem, of being a victim, and of having no choices in life. Mindfulness and meditation, living in the 'now', finding body awareness, connections between brain and body and body-based grounding techniques were all helpful and led me to question my faith and theology. Some of these techniques are now integrating into my prayer life. I began to comprehend the true wonder of 'love God and love your neighbour *as you love yourself*'.

There was much change, much loss and much gain. Losses made space for the new, as I understood former learned stereotypical beliefs, and began to slowly alter these. My theology and faith changed completely. I realised with great joy but also more pain that I was responsible for much more in my life than had ever occurred to me. Others could not in reality *make* me feel anything – I could choose my feelings and whether I responded or reacted to life. Changing from victim mode was scary, threatening, liberating, sometimes easy and sometimes indomitably challenging.

My discoveries of liberal theology and indeed of Inclusive Church were breakthrough moments. I realised how important inclusion in the church was for me and for those who encounter the marginalisation of mental health issues. Additionally it was brought home to me that on many occasions and in many places the church is not understanding, welcoming, empathic; it is neither embracing nor is it a safe, loving place for those many who journey with mental health issues. Understanding is sometimes trapped in long-inappropriate associations of mental health with evil.

Liturgy is often marred by an overemphasis on shame, guilt, unworthiness and sin, already too close to home for those who journey with mental health issues. The church's dualistic attitude towards light and dark is not always helpful – darkness can be a very safe place for those of us who encounter mental health issues. Sometimes the language of hymns can be unhelpful and judgemental, even in those resources considered to be particularly appropriate: for example, in 'Amazing Grace' about saving a 'wretch', or 'Dear Lord and Father' with 'forgive our foolish ways; re-clothe us in our rightful mind'.

We all are God's beloved children, not wretches; foolishness and mental-health are not linked; we who journey with those issues are not necessarily out of our rightful minds. We need more self-love, self-affirmation, reminders that God's love is unconditional and non-judgemental. The language of healing and wholeness can sometimes forget that God is present in paradox, present in fragmentation, present in darkness, in shadow and light, and that healing and wholeness can encompass a theology of community embracing community wherever they are, of individual embracing individual wherever he or she is. The journey from exclusion to inclusion has at least begun. Increased awareness is needed.

PART 2

Theology

A Place to Belong – understanding and being alongside people experiencing mental health problems
JEAN VANIER AND JOHN SWINTON

Each book in this series contains a substantial theological reflection by an expert in the field. Here Jean Vanier and John Swinton help us reflect theologically about mental health issues. They both write from their wide experience, encouraging us to help create a church that is more than inclusive, a church where all people belong.

JEAN VANIER is one of the world's most respected philosopher-theologians, and founder of L'Arche, an international organisation that creates communities where people with intellectual disabilities and those who assist them share life together.

JOHN SWINTON is Chair in Divinity and Religious Studies at the University of Aberdeen and an expert in disability theology and pastoral care. He is a former mental health nurse and mental health chaplain.

CHAPTER 1

Reclaiming the 'specialness' of the church

> "'Love the Lord your God with all your heart and with all your soul and with all your strength and with all your mind"; and, "Love your neighbour as yourself."'
>
> (Luke 10:27)

I (Jean) was touched when Inclusive Church asked me to contribute to a book on the theology of mental illness. My 50 years of experience in L'Arche living alongside people with intellectual disabilities has opened me up to an understanding of the experience of people suffering from various forms of mental disorder. By that I do not mean to imply that intellectual disabilities and mental illnesses are the same thing. They are not, and it is important that that separation is made clear from the start, not for fear of one stigmatising the other, but simply because they are different experiences which should not be conflated. What unites those with mental illnesses and those with intellectual disabilities is that each of them needs to be welcomed, appreciated, loved, understood and listened to with respect. They need to belong. Unfortunately this is exactly how people often *do not* feel. The shared pain and the place of meeting between people with mental illnesses and people with intellectual disabilities is the collective experience of being rejected and often despised; of being seen as different or mad, foolish or crazy. It is this shared pain that creates ways of being in the world which prevent both groups of people from advancing and growing into the maturity and the beauty that they have the potential to achieve. Over the years some of the people with disabilities with whom I have lived have experienced various forms of mental illness. So mental illness has always been on my horizon, though I claim no specialist expertise.

Some of the people who have lived in our communities were diagnosed with serious mental illnesses in childhood. They were placed in our community at the age of 20 after many years of being rejected and often despised, seen as different or mad, foolish or crazy. Over time they have become perfectly adapted to our community life. Their experiences of mental illness often remain, but they are happy living with us and being held within our structured life. Those who came to be with us after experiencing painful crises and serious mental illnesses sometimes had more difficulties. Many were unable to live our life in community and we had to find a more suitable place for them. But others have found our communities to be safe places. People experience depression, personality issues and other mental disturbances; but they also find relief and release as they learn what it means to be loved and accepted in community: *to belong*. This idea of *belonging* runs like a golden thread through our book. If the church has anything to offer to people with mental illness (and indeed to anyone else), it is the provision of a space where they can truly feel that they belong. We hope that this book will help to begin to open up such a space.

In contributing to this book I am wary of attempting to enter into the domain of mental illness. While I may have something to say on the core issues, I am not a professional theologian, a psychiatrist or a specialist in the field of mental illness. I found peace, trust and the confidence to attempt to write on this subject when John Swinton accepted my invitation to write with me. I needed someone who was a real specialist in this domain to co-author the work. John is a theologian who has many years of experience walking alongside people with mental illnesses, both as a mental health nurse and as a chaplain working with people living with mental illnesses. We felt that together we could produce something that was hopeful, helpful and, perhaps, transforming.

The tyranny of the normal

Our society wants people to fit in; to go to school like everyone else, to get a job, to relate to others harmoniously; to be the same. Our societies have difficulty with people who are perceived as different. At one time it was religious orders who sought to break through the barriers of difference and offer care and tenderness to those rejected as strangers and outcasts. For many years, perhaps even centuries, those who needed different forms of specialised help (those with mental illness, those considered to be mentally disabled, the sick, the poor etc.), found consolation by being cared for by *special* religious people; religious people who were *special* in their motivations, tenderness, compassion, if not always in their competence! Today things are different. There are fewer religious people, but there are more 'specialists': psychiatrists, mental health nurses, social workers, special educators, therapists and so on. There has been progress in accepting people who are different. Now there are many different types of schools, workshops, residences and services, all designed to facilitate rehabilitation and help people find community and peacefulness. This is all for the good.

It is interesting to note the way in which the term 'special', with regard to mental health care, seems to have moved from the religious to the secular. The temptation is to think that religion nowadays has nothing much to offer in the face of so many specialists! Religion sometimes seems a little strange in the face of the technological specialties we find in mental health services. But of course religious communities have much to offer if they can find the confidence to offer it. Our hope in writing this short book is that religious communities can regain their confidence and reclaim their special ministry towards one particular group of marginalised people.

As we marvel at the rise of the specialists in mental health care, we can easily forget the small things. People suffering from severe mental illnesses can become completely lost in the midst of the bureaucracy that accompanies the administration of complex treatments and changes occurring in the system. The complicated paperwork that people have to complete in order to receive their benefits is often far too convoluted. There are far too few residences and places of respite. The temptation simply to hand out medication and do little more is ever present in the midst of a busy and overburdened health care service. Many of those who are sick live with a lot of suffering and difficulties in their family or on their own. Some fall into street life; they disturb society. People feel lost when they are in contact with them, not because people with mental illness are not lovable, but because people have learned the wrong stories to tell about them. Some gravitate towards churches or church organisations, sensing that there they may find some compassion and help. Sometimes they do, but often they don't.

Here we touch on the heart of this book. What does the church have to do to reclaim its 'specialness'? The answer is both complicated and simple at the same time: *the churches' call is to meet those with mental illness, to learn to love them with the love and the passion of Jesus and to offer them a place of belonging.* It is in these small and apparently foolish things that Jesus will be revealed (1 Cor. 1:27). John and

I hope that this book may help church people to be more confident about their 'specialness' and to be enabled to look differently at the experience of mental illness, and in looking differently see properly. When we see properly we act faithfully.

How we wrote this book

Readers may be interested in the process through which these next chapters were written. Our contribution to the book emerges from our longstanding friendship. Although written by us both, the reader should read it as a single essay. We are sure that those who know our work will go through it saying, 'Oh! That is Jean!' or, 'Oh! That is John!' But we would urge the reader not to think in such ways. We have written these chapters together. Each chapter is a weaving together of both of our thoughts and perspectives; a tapestry of ideas that has emerged from our shared experience and passion to help the church to walk faithfully and peaceably together in all of its beautiful diversity. Rather than trying to work out who wrote what and why, we would urge you simply to meditate on the ideas and not to let curiosity distract you from the vital truths and transformative possibilities that, we hope, we can draw to your attention.

CHAPTER 2

The mission of Jesus and the lives of people with mental illness

[I am writing] to all who have been
called by God the Father, who loves you
and keeps you safe in the care of Jesus
Christ.

(Jude 1:1)

The Gospels reveal a Jesus who is
compassionate and humble of heart. He came
to liberate everybody from those forces of
sinfulness which incite people to violence
and hatred and which separate them behind
walls of fear. He came to announce a God who
loves every person and calls them to unity
and to peace. Among the great divisions is the
one that separates the poor and the rich. He
calls the rich to dispossess themselves and
share with those who are in need; he calls
those who are rejected and lonely to hope and
reveals to them that they are precious to God.

We see Jesus forgiving, healing and helping people in need. People brought Jesus 'all the sick, those afflicted with various diseases and pains, demoniacs, epileptics, and paralytics, and he healed them' (Matt. 4:24). He puts as requirements for entry into the Kingdom of God (Matt. 25) compassion, giving food and drink to the hungry and thirsty, visiting the sick and those in prison, welcoming strangers.

For disciples of Jesus it is not just a matter of preaching and telling people in distress that they are loved by God. To be a disciple is to say to those in need, 'I love you and want to be committed to you, in order to help you to be liberated from rejection, and find the appropriate help as together we move towards peace and love.' Such discipleship reveals the message of Jesus by living it. For disciples, there can be no separation between life and words (James 2). Those with mental illness may well *be* such disciples. But they also need to be able to find and interact with other disciples within our churches; people who seek to *meet* with them; to *understand* them, to *appreciate* them, to *love* them and to reveal to them that they are loved by God. Meeting, understanding, appreciating and loving – such is the way of the Kingdom. Such a loving dynamic is not a one-way thing; it is not a gift that the church alone offers to people with mental illness. It is also a gift that churches need to learn to accept *from* people living with mental illnesses.

As disciples, we recognise that our hearts of stone must then be transformed into hearts of flesh, pure hearts that are vulnerable and loving. This is not simply an act of human beings; it is a gift of the Spirit. Ezekiel says, 'I will give you a new heart and put a new spirit in you; I will remove from you your heart of stone and give you a heart of flesh' (Ezek. 36:26). Disciples of Jesus are not called to be competent therapists, but to have hearts that are understanding and loving. Growing into love is a long, hard road (1 Cor. 13:4–7). Patience, kindness, perseverance, forgiveness and hope, all take time. Love takes time. Such love is given to us by the Holy Spirit, just as Jesus promised. The message of Jesus is not merely a law that must be obeyed. If it were, the weak and the rejected would quickly feel guilty, unworthy, fearful of punishment, as indeed all persons would. Jesus came with a deep love designed to draw into his loving arms all those who have a broken image of themselves: those who are depressed and feel unloved; those who are sad in their spirits, but loved in their souls. He came with love to save and liberate those who are not able to live the law. Jesus brings to us a spirit of graceful love; a form of

64

love that is not determined by human action (or the lack of it), but is motivated and driven by the desire to reach out to the wounded, the rejected and the weak. The open arms of Jesus on the cross draw all into his graceful loving presence. Recognising this is the beginning of discipleship and the point at which the churches' 'specialness' begins to reveal itself.

It is only as we learn to love with the grace and compassion of Jesus that the suggestion that the wounded and the rejected can find places of welcome within our churches, our church halls, our retreat homes and our own hearts can become a possibility. Only then can those with deep psychological afflictions begin to believe that they are loved by God and can live a relationship of friendship with Jesus alongside those who claim to follow him. Only when the church can be *seen* to be the church can people be persuaded that it *is* the church. The love of Jesus has to be seen to be believed. The beginning point for the church's ministry alongside people with mental illness is the recognition of the power of graceful love. In a special way people with mental illnesses need to hear, see and feel the message of the love, acceptance and graceful forgiveness of Jesus.

Forgiveness

Forgiveness is at the heart, of the gospel message. Many people experiencing mental illnesses can end up blaming themselves for their situation. 'Is my illness caused by something I have done?' 'Should I do something or stop doing something?' 'Is God punishing me?' People can feel that their disturbances and strange experiences, their suicide attempts, their depressions and perhaps even their violence have caused pain to themselves, their family and friends. Feelings of guilt can devour people. The beauty of the gospel is that forgiveness is available to all, free of charge! Forgiveness is healing. In the light of the cross we can come close and whisper to one another: 'God is not punishing you.' 'You have an illness.' 'You need not pressurise yourself by trying to do things differently. People will help you. People love you.' 'It may well be that you have caused distress to others, but Jesus forgives you.' People need to discover the open arms of Jesus as he gently calls them to a relationship of love within which they can believe and experience the fact that they are free, forgiven, and that, as the apostle Paul says, 'nothing can ever separate us from God's love' (Rom. 8:39). The task of the church is to embody that love in order that those who are broken can feel such love. This is the theological foundation of our call to love.

The pain of people with mental illness: listening and understanding

It is difficult for an outsider to speak of the pain that people with mental illness experience. Both Jean and John have seen and been moved by chronically ill people in psychiatric wards strutting up and down a hospital ward muttering to themselves and clearly distressed. How can we understand if we have not walked with them? Where is their hope? A young woman at college who suddenly experiences a major life crisis is given medication. A little later she throws it away because of the side-effects. She begins to scream in the middle of the street, frightened of being hurt by imaginary thugs; she is taken away by the police. The temptation is simply to distance ourselves by saying 'she is ill'. In this way we pass the responsibility to the 'specialists' and in so doing abrogate ourselves of responsibility. But we cannot know how she feels. We cannot truly understand what she is experiencing. We cannot judge her because we do not know. But if we were to take time and listen to what she is going through, perhaps we could understand her? Instead of passing

her on to the 'specialists', perhaps our job is
to learn how to come close and listen to her;
to learn how to value her experience and love
and understand her? Perhaps muttering has
meaning.

Jean remembers being touched and
saddened by a person who, having lived through
a clinical depression said to him, 'Nobody could
understand me; I felt I was in a snake pit.' As
Jean listened he did begin to understand. He
could never claim: 'I know how you feel!' And
nor should he. But he could listen and try to
understand what the other was going through.
Again, there are those who become lost in the
midst of Alzheimer's disease. They no longer
seem to be able to understand where they are
or even who they are; they feel totally lost.
How are we to accompany them? People who
have bipolar disorder can quickly move from
depression to hysterical enthusiasm; nobody
seems to understand them, they feel rejected.
Alongside of their chaotic inner pain and
anguish, people with mental illness often have
the additional pain of feeling that nobody can
understand them, and in frightening ways
they cannot understand themselves. They may
feel unwanted by God and unloved by everyone
around them. This leads to a deep vulnerability
which easily leads to mistreatment, abuse and a

lack of sensitivity to people's experiences, even by doctors and medical staff. Those in so-called 'normal' society are fearful of strangeness and difference and can be intolerant and excluding, leading to loneliness and isolation.

And yet, Jesus calls us to engage in persistent love; a love that is gentle, kind, loving and patient. Such love takes time. And time is exactly what many of us are tempted *not* to offer to people with mental illnesses. When we slow down and take time to listen and try to understand, things begin to look different. When people who are mentally ill cry out or draw attention to themselves in the midst of their sadness or confusion, it may be that these expressions of concern are not actually 'problems'. They may be the expression of experiences, questions, fears, requests for love. Might it not be that they are looking for someone who, at last, will see them as persons and will listen to them? The real problem may be that we have not yet learned the practice of listening properly; of slowing down, being patient and opening our souls to the confusion of the other. Maybe the experiences of mentally ill people are not just problems to be solved? Perhaps they are in fact cries to be heard, respected, trusted and understood: cries that demand love.

The task of the church is to listen and to

try to understand; to hear people through the confusion and to move towards those who weep. There is a temptation, for some of us, to move away from people with mental illnesses for fear of being engulfed by their pain. We are afraid that we will end up getting lost among the lost. We feel inadequate, incapable of dealing with the situation. Instead of moving forward in love, we retreat backwards in fear. However, 'There is no fear in love. Indeed, perfect love drives out fear' (1 John 4:18). The call of Jesus is to hear the cries for love and to move forwards in friendship and in perseverant love; a mode of friendship which destroys stigma and opens up space for all of us together to be fully human even in the midst of our wildest storms.

If this is so, then the church is not called to find cures for the problem of mental illness. Such a task belongs to specialists of a different kind. It is called to a ministry of *listening*, *understanding* and *spiritual consolation*. Many people with mental illnesses retain hope in the midst of their pain, anguish and inner chaos; a hope that they will meet with God, a meeting that is mediated, for better and for worse, in and through God's disciples. Taking time to listen and to understand is not complicated: a look of respect, a gesture of love and tenderness, a thoughtful word that will reveal to people that they are not forgotten by God (or by humans); that they are loved. It is in the small things of this world that the Kingdom of God is revealed.

The presence of God in mental illness: recognising the small things

Jean remembers a psychiatrist friend telling him that many people who are in serious psychotic states can remain open to authentic and deeply meaningful relationships. He told me of a patient who was claiming to be Jesus. He listened to him without contradiction or discussion. When the man stopped talking, Jean's friend said to him, 'If you want, I can give you some medication which might relieve some of your pain.' The ill man agreed and accepted the medication. Obviously he knew he was ill, and like so many people with mental illness, he wanted to feel better. He was also in front of a man – the psychiatrist – who was clearly a man of compassion who listened to him respectfully and took him seriously. It is in such little openings into respect and relationship that the possibility of encountering 'real persons' rather than diagnoses can occur. Such small things are the physical manifestations of belonging.

Louis who is 45 years old gave this witness during a conference on disabilities and society.

He presented himself as 'a schizophrenic'. The first symptoms appeared when he was 20. There followed long years of suffering. He spoke of the terrible anguish that overcame him, the crises, the violence and the uncontrollable acts which eventually brought him to be hospitalised. He spoke of his terrible solitude and loneliness. Louis was angry. Who could blame him? He was treated with revulsion by his family and friends who disappeared in fear, not knowing what to do. He was like the psalmist who cried out, 'You have caused my friends to abandon me; you have made me repulsive to them. I am closed in and cannot escape' (Ps. 88:8). Now, with distance, he realises that such experiences, terrible as they were, were only for a season. Today, with the help of the right medication and the support of others, he is pretty well stabilised. Louis has learned to anticipate crises; he knows his personal flashpoints and he knows where and how to find appropriate help. He told the audience:

In the worst moments of my illness and during the horrible crises I always felt a faithful presence of the Virgin Mary. I was certain that she would never leave me. Often I felt she was with me as she was with Jesus during the way of the cross. That gave me a lot of peace. But when I told this to a few people nobody took it seriously; in fact they imagined that was all part of my illness! I kept it secretly in my own heart. For a long time I hoped that Jesus would heal me. My real healing is that I have now accepted my illness and become more open to other people.

Louis reminds us of two things. First, the tragedy of Louis's story is the way in which his label of being mentally ill shadowed everything that he did and thought. It is a grotesque tragedy when meaningful spiritual experiences are explained away as being 'just another aspect of his illness'. Second, Louis reminds us that we must never see just illness in a mentally ill person: we must not allow the person to be subsumed to the illness. Even those things that we call 'illness' have meaning if we are prepared to look properly and listen without bias. There is a very real spiritual life within each person, even though it may at times be hidden beneath the turmoil of our lives. In each of us there is a secret. It is within this secret that Jesus lives.

Dr Nancy Kehoe has written a fascinating book about the spiritual and religious life of chronically ill people. She is a psychotherapist and a nun who suggested starting a discussion group on religion within the psychiatric hospital where she worked. She brought together a group of patients and gave them an opportunity to share and discuss their religious and spiritual experiences. The other doctors and therapists at the hospital were hesitant, partly because they felt that religion was somehow bad for people with mental health issues and partly because most of them were atheists or agnostics. In the end they accepted the 'experiment'. The book reveals how people with severe mental illness can have and can ably articulate real spiritual experiences, and are often keen to speak of them. Many of them wanted to know about prayer: does God listen to them? Others wanted to feel protected by God, and to wear a religious symbol to remind them of God's presence. Some wanted to speak of the church they used to go to, or about their parents who had died. All needed to speak about what they deemed as their most intimate secrets, which they dared not share with doctors or therapists or even, normally, with other patients. Religion was important to them even if those who offered care to them seemed to think otherwise.

True spiritual experiences like Louis's

and the participants in Nancy Kehoe's group are spoken of in humble ways. There is no need for complex spiritual exercises. They just happen when people come close to God and one another. As they come close there is no need to deny their illness; it becomes part of who they are and where they have been; part of their formation. In this way the person is helped to accept their illness without denying their spirituality, and in so doing is enabled to find new ways of encountering relational healing. Psychosis, sadness and confusion can lead to denial: 'I am not really ill!' When this happens people are cut off from reality and from others. What we see in the stories above is the simple fact that expressing true spiritual experiences can bring people back to a place of confidence, value and acceptance: a place of healing. The importance for a disciple of Jesus is to listen with respect to people who are ill, to help them realise that the person behind the illness is important, and that above all else they are loved by God.

Both Jean and John have been deeply moved by the holiness and humility of some of the mentally ill people that they have known. Many have not had any deep religious experiences like the one Louis had, but they have accepted both that they are ill and that their illness has meaning beyond the mere desire to get rid of it. They know who to go to in times of crisis; they meet regularly with their doctor and they know they must keep on with their medication. They live a life that is regular and without excesses and they are careful not to let themselves get into situations which could create anguish in them. They have learned how to live and accept themselves as they are. Like Louis, they are no longer seeking a cure; they desire to live life in all of its fullness, alongside of and in the midst of their illness. Jesus came to bring life in all of its fullness. The challenge for the church is to ask and to answer the question: what does that look like?

CHAPTER 3

Meeting people with mental illnesses

'I have come that they may have life,
and have it to the full.'

(John 10:10)

In the light of what has been said, it has
become clear that the church's special task of
walking with people who have mental illness
is not focused on *curing*. God may choose
to cure people, but that is not the churches'
primary responsibility. The key task of the
church is to enable *healing*. Curing relates to
the eradication of an illness or a disease. But
healing is something different; something
deeper, more soulful. To be cured one needs to
be rid of one's disease. But to be healed, one
needs to learn how to live well with it. Healing
has to do with how we find health in the midst
of our illnesses. Healing has to do with finding
wholeness, inner beauty, unity and peace.
In the Bible, such wholeness is described as

shalom. It is interesting to notice that the Bible has no word for health in the way that we often use the term. Shalom is not the *absence* of illness. Rather it is the *presence* of God. Shalom means righteousness and holiness; right relationship with God. To experience shalom is to be in right relationship with God irrespective of the state of our bodies or minds. *To be healthy is to love God in all things and at all times.* John remembers talking on the idea of shalom at a mental health conference. After he had talked, a man came up to him and said, 'You know, I have never heard of that idea before. I have had a mental illness for most of my life. I love Jesus. But I thought that the reason I was unwell was because I was a bad Christian. Now I see things differently.' Jesus is the bearer of shalom (Eph. 2:14). Shalom is the key to understanding health in the midst of illness. The call of the church is to help people experiencing mental illnesses to find healing, to encounter God's shalom.

Meeting is healing

Thus far we have seen the importance of listening, striving to understand, being patient, taking time and embodying the love of Jesus. These are the small gestures of the Kingdom that bring about healing. In this chapter we want to continue to develop our model of caring, healing discipleship by thinking through what it means to *meet* with people who have mental illness. Meeting one another is difficult in a world that has taken on board the madness of individualism, which has led to a deep sense of existential loneliness that is manifested sharply in the alienation of the weak, but that touches all of us. As we learn to communicate more (internet, Twitter, Facebook, Instagram, etc.), so our relationships have become more fragile. The idea of unfriending those who trouble us easily transfers from Facebook to communities of flesh and blood. Meeting one another is never easy. It becomes all the more difficult when those whom we desire to meet may, at times, see the world quite differently from ourselves.

Meeting one another well is a work of the Spirit. It has to do with receiving the gift of the Spirit which leads us into love, a divine love that respects and values difference. Such a gift helps us to see that in Jesus 'there is no longer Jew or Gentile, slave or free, male and female [mentally well or mentally ill]. For you are all one in Christ Jesus' (Gal. 3:28). It is in and through the Spirit that we are enabled to meet one another as we are, rather than as we might like one another to be. Meeting one another well produces moments of communion that occur in the space between us; a space that is inhabited by both of us; a space that is saturated with graceful love. In this space, neither one nor the other is superior. It is a place where we meet in humility, and love without judgement; just two people, recognising the other as precious and important; two human beings desiring to be present for one to another.

Tony

One afternoon in a railway station in Paris, Jean felt himself drawn to talk with a man he saw sitting on his own. The man was around 30 years old and his face was lined by dirt and suffering. At his feet there was a huge dog. The man was begging. Jean went up to him, shook his hand and asked what his name was. 'Tony,' he replied. He was from Paris. We talked for a little bit. Jean said, 'I am sorry. I have nothing to give you. I am not in any way capable of helping you to find a job or anything like that.' Tony looked at Jean and smiled. 'I've been standing here for many long hours and nobody has looked at me during all of that time. *You looked at me.*' He smiled and said 'Thank you'. Jean was touched and moved. In some ways we were just two poor human beings meeting by chance. But in other ways we were both

teachers. Tony revealed to me my humanity
and I think/hope that I also revealed his
humanity to him. I looked at him. In those brief
moments we were brothers, linked together as
kin, recognising our common bonds within the
same human family. I believe that we met.
What was most beautiful in him and in myself
was that our humanness came together in a
certain oneness; a moment of peace, an instant
of shalom, was given to each of us. Within
that moment we understood what it meant to
be human in the presence of one another and
through the Spirit of God. We were present one
to another: we met.

Pauline

The L'Arche community in Trosly welcomed
Pauline in 1970. Pauline was 40 at that time.
She had hemiplegia and suffered from epilepsy.
One of her arms and one leg was paralysed.
She was an angry person who was prone to
unexpected outbursts of shouting and breaking
things. She was obviously mentally disturbed
and not an easy person to get along with. In our
small homes it is not easy to live with someone
like Pauline, no matter how much we might
desire to love her. Our psychiatrist helped us to
find ways of pacifying Pauline. He told us that
the reason for her violence was not mysterious.

The cause of her violence was many years of humiliation and lack of respect. Her family had been, and continued to be, ashamed of her. She was mocked in the streets by strangers, laughed at and despised by her peers at school. No wonder she hated her body! It was the source of all her difficulties. No wonder she hated herself. How can you love yourself when everyone around you seems to hate you? Our psychiatrist helped us to see, accept and appreciate her in a different way: as a hurting, troubled person who needed to be loved. Underneath all of her confusion, anger and violence, her human heart yearned to be loved. Her violence and her screams were a language; they were distorted ways of asking, 'Does anyone love me?' The manifestations of her troubles were a call for someone to trust her and see her as someone precious and in need of friendship. No judging, no criticising, no controlling, no domineering, only open friendship that would enable her to meet others.

One thing that has become clear over the years is that for some of the assistants who come to L'Arche such an attitude of meeting and friendship doesn't immediately seem to make sense. 'Did we not come to do good to people with disabilities?' Such an assumption implies a certain superiority. In order to accept Pauline as she was, to call forth her real person, required a real humility and an openness to a new vision of the human person as precious. As we deal with precious people it soon becomes clear that we are no longer governed by fear, prejudices and false sentiments of superiority. It is only through meetings of mutual help, authentic meetings in everyday life, that we come to know who we really are. As we engaged in frivolous fun and laughter, little by little we were given the gift of seeing the person of Pauline emerge. These assistants needed help to meet the real self of Pauline hidden behind her violence. They needed to grow humanly and spiritually; their minds needed to be softened and taught not to 'conform to the pattern of this world, but be transformed by the renewing of [their minds]' (Rom. 12:2). This could only be done through and in a community and with the help of the Holy Spirit. It was only as the assistants met with Pauline that such transformation could occur.

How quickly we can say, 'It is not my problem.' Jesus wants to transform us so that we have hearts like his, fleshy, warm and loving. Jesus wants our hearts, hearts that are so often closed up in fear, closed up in ourselves and in our comfort and security, to change and open us up to others. The greatest pain of people with mental illness is to be seen as different, to be stigmatised as 'abnormal', pushed away into a horrible world of loneliness, isolation, anguish and pain; trapped in a space where no one desires to meet with them. The call of the church is a simple one: *meet people where they are.*

Beyond stigma: the power of meeting

St Francis in his Testament says that he was repulsed by people who were suffering from leprosy: repulsed by their fragmented bodies, the smell of open wounds filled with pus. One day he felt called by Jesus to be with them, to meet with them. He heard that call and he stayed with them and cared for them. We can understand the fears of Francis; leprosy at that time was contagious. There was the terrible pain of the sickness in these men and women, but there was also the pain of rejection and exclusion. Francis must have experienced people's joy when people recognised his desire to meet them. The task of the church is to meet people and, in meeting them, enable their joy. Perhaps the most devastating aspect of mental illness is the stigma that is associated with it. The idea of stigma emerges from the slave trade. When a slave-owner bought a slave the slave was given a brand. This was the mark of the slave master. It meant that the person was no longer a person; now she was nothing more than a brand. For mentally ill people, stigma reduces the person to the shape and size of their diagnosis. We saw how this masked the real person and their spirituality when we reflected on Louis's story earlier. Meeting people in love destroys stigma and gives the person back their name. Pauline's story embodies this. As our minds were renewed, we began to realise that Pauline was no longer a 'nuisance' or someone who was 'deeply disturbed'. As we met, so we learned to recognise that Pauline was ... well ... *Pauline*! – someone to be valued, loved and respected for who she is and the transformative gifts she had to share with us. Meeting destroys stigma and resurrects persons.

Growing in the love of Jesus and in openness to the Holy Spirit

In our communities of L'Arche, we have noted that assistants living with people like Pauline need to find a special force which enables them to remain patient, kind, persevering and able to bear and endure all. This force is given as assistants enter into personal friendships. This force is an inner strength which is manifested in *tenderness*: the tenderness of a true relationship.

Tenderness is an amazing capacity. Tenderness means listening with compassion to people's stories and their suffering; it means meeting and welcoming another person with gentleness and care, offering understanding without the desire to dominate or to teach. To act tenderly is to call forth and welcome the gift of the other, as we, in turn, offer our gift. Tenderness implies mutual trust and humility. Isn't tenderness really a gift of the Holy Spirit which flows from the tenderness of a God who is tender? Tenderness destroys stigma and restores personhood. Tenderness is a revelation of discipleship carried out in the Spirit.

Maybe we will end up saying, 'I am sorry I can do nothing for you, but I want you to know that we care for you.' 'Maybe we can put you in touch with somebody who can help?' Such an admission is the beginning point for healing. Maybe doing absolutely nothing is what needs to be done? *Being* rather than *doing* may be the key to meeting those with difficult mental experiences. We offer tea and biscuits: hospitality. We talk a little; take time to learn and to receive the hospitality of *strangers*. We learn to live one another's pain and share one another's alienation. Real meeting means being willing to feel lost with those who feel lost and using the sharing of our lostness as the basis of communion. As the song goes, 'I once was lost but now I'm found.' This is the heart of compassionate meeting; an amazing grace!

The grace of L'Arche

The amazing grace within L'Arche is that assistants live out and experience a certain transformation as they enter into communion with people like Pauline. They experience something very deep. Those they had considered as the lowest in the hierarchy of humanity, those who are frequently put away, hidden in institutions and humiliated are the ones who lead them into a new vision of humanness. Those who are weak and rejected can teach us that happiness or the fulfilment of a person is not in rising higher in promotion, in wealth, in power, in recognition and in a social status or in doing good. True happiness occurs when we learn to see one another properly. It occurs when we learn to develop a true love of people who are in one sense different – different cultures, religions, sicknesses, disabilities – and yet at a deeper level very much the same. People are people. If we, individually or as societies, forget that, we easily forget the humanness of the ill, the disabled and the stigmatised. Martin Buber notices the strange tension between good and evil. In order to love someone we need to move towards them; to reach out and do something. However, in order to do evil, we just have to not think about things. A lesson of the Holocaust is that evil comes from thoughtlessness, a turning away from the obvious and a refusal to think about it. Stigma easily drifts into evil. Love overcomes. Genuine mental health care begins by thinking properly about the humanness and the beauty of people with mental illnesses.

Life in the Spirit

In John 14, Jesus promises to pray to the Father, who will send us another Paraclete, the Spirit of truth, to be always with us if we love him and keep his commandments. And the commandment of Jesus, a new one, which he repeats clearly four times in John, is that we love one another as he loves us. In the Gospel of Luke (6:27) Jesus insists that we are called to love our enemies; to love as he loves, and wash the feet of others as he washed the feet of his disciples. This means that we must not remain closed up in our group, culture or even in our own churches, seeking glory and domination over others. We should not remain behind protective walls where we defend our way of believing, thinking, living, praying and so on, seeking to 'convert' people to our own group or way of thinking. When we close ourselves off from others, we risk being unable then to follow the Holy Spirit; unable to be open to others, unable to learn from them, and receive the gifts of God from them. Such love is not a prison that cuts us off from others, but a gentle stream that cleanses us and opens our minds to the fullness of Jesus' promise that 'God so loved the world that he gave his only son.' Discipleship opens us to the fullness of God's grace and the uniqueness of God's son. We are called to love others as Jesus loves them and to be a fountain of love for them.

Of course, loving the world in such ways is not easy! It means loving those who seem not to be like us – those with different views, those who are not friendly and open. Indeed it even means loving our enemies! Jesus says it is easy to love those who love us; to love those who seem to be different is more complicated. However, what is clear from our discussion thus far is that people with mental illnesses only *seem* to be different. If it is true that 'people are just people', then compulsions, delusions, depression, anxiety and all of the different experiences that people go through may be better understood if we come close rather than back off; if we meet rather than retreat. When we come close we will realise that our fears may be unfounded. As we learn to love one another in the midst of our storms, we may discover that love reveals persons and that those persons are more like us than not like us. It may well be that the task of the psychiatrist is to bring cure and relieve symptoms. But, if what we have written in this book is correct, then the primary task of the church is to love and to heal without the demand for cure. More than that, we are called to be courageous in our love; to refuse to bow to the false delusions of stigma and to reach out and rescue those whose personhood is being destroyed, not by mental illness but by people's responses to what they think mental illness is and implies.

The primary gift that the church has to offer is the creation of a graceful space for meeting within which the possibility of listening, understanding, friendship, belonging and tenderness becomes real. To love is to see the other as a gift. For this we need the gift of the Spirit. To see the poor and the needy, the disabled and the mentally ill not only as people 'we' can help and to whom 'we' can do good, but rather as people with whom all people desire to share communion and who can offer new life and refreshed minds. Our hearts of stone need to be transformed into hearts of flesh. We need to grow into love in the power of the Holy Spirit.

Who am I?

In one of his richest prison poems Dietrich Bonhoeffer helps us all to discover that our real identity is to belong to Jesus. Writing from prison Bonhoeffer asks the question, 'Who am I? Am I the person who in prison is seen as peaceful and strong and about whom everybody is saying how wonderful you are? Or am I that weak person inside of me who is filled with fears and with anguish?' Bonhoeffer ends with a prayer to Jesus: 'Above all,' he says, 'I belong to you, I am thine.' Our real identity is not then in our church group, our diagnosis, our feelings about ourselves or how other people perceive and act towards us. Who we are is found in Jesus. God knows who I am! It is through Jesus that people with mental illness can find the strength to hold onto hope. It is in Jesus that we discover renewed inner strength to love others whom we may perceive as different. It is because of Jesus that we are freed to love.

Etty Hillesum says in her diary, 'I discover that I am in a well. At the bottom of this well there is a presence of God but frequently I cannot attain this presence because of the rocks and the garbage and all sorts of things which stop me meeting him.' These rocks and garbage are all those things of which we need to be purified, all those fears we have of other people, our lack of love, the ways we judge and condemn others, our aggression and our violence and our incapacity to forgive our fear of those who are different. We need to be purified of all these blocks so that we can be truly open to the Spirit and love people as Jesus loves them. This means that our church group should never be a prison but always a fountain that calls us to be more deeply in communion with Jesus and with others.

We need to be disarmed of those certitudes, assumptions and stereotypes which close us in upon ourselves and upon our group. As we are freed of the need to be the best, or seeing others as 'no good', and also wanting ourselves to have the last word, so we become disciples. The late Patriarch of Constantinople, Athenagoras, wrote in an article: 'The hardest war is a war against oneself; we have to arrive at renunciation. I waged this war for years and it was terrible, now I'm disarmed I no longer fear anything because love chases fear away.' This informs us that we are always to be attentive and close to those who are different, not trying to judge or to condemn them. They too are children of God, with their own stories and their own set of hopes, dreams and expectations. When we begin to think in such ways, truly meeting with one another becomes real.

A few years ago Jean was invited to Chile. He was met at the airport by Denis who drove him to Santiago. At one moment on the way, as they turned a curve, he told Jean, 'On the left are the huge slums of Santiago; on the right are all the homes of rich people, protected by the police and the military.' He added, 'Nobody ever crosses this road'; everybody is frightened. *They never meet.* A real meeting comes when we risk approaching those whom we assume to be different, perhaps even our enemies. To meet is to approach others with the desire for peace and unity. It is to live out and into the commandment to love. As we meet, the Holy Spirit transforms an awkward moment into a meeting of peace where each one is transformed. God is present in the meeting. This implies that disciples of Jesus are not afraid of feeling incapable and lost in front of people experiencing mental illness. Likewise those disciples who love Jesus and experience mental illness can find a place of meeting where their faith is upheld, valued and sustained, and the experiences that they are having can be heard and valued in ways that are transformative and healing.

CHAPTER 4

Giving people back their names

> He brought them to the man to see what
> he would name them; and whatever the
> man called each living creature, that
> was its name.
>
> (Gen. 2:19)

The church is not called to become a community
of psychiatrists; it is called to become a
community of persistent, patient love.
Psychiatry and the mental health professions
have their place. But their tasks are different
(although complementary) from the tasks of
the church. The church's task is to give people
back their names.

In Genesis 2:19–20, Adam is given
responsibility to name God's creatures:

> Now the Lord God had formed out of
> the ground all the wild animals and
> all the birds in the sky. He brought
> them to the man to see what he would

> name them; and whatever the man
> called each living creature, that was its
> name. So the man gave names to all the
> livestock, the birds in the sky and all
> the wild animals.

Whatever name Adam gave to the animals that became its name. Tigers became tigers and sheep became sheep, as and when Adam named them. Naming, then, is a primary responsibility of human beings. The act of naming has creative power: it brings things into existence.

The act of naming is a central vocation for human beings. It is also central to our understanding of faithful discipleship. In John 15:14–17 Jesus renames his followers in a deep and profound way. He says to his disciples, 'I no longer call you servants, because a servant does not know his master's business. Instead, I have called you friends, for everything that I learned from my Father I have made known to you.' In this profound act of naming, Jesus brings into existence something radically new and quite beautiful. No longer were they servants, now they were friends; friends with Jesus, the incarnated one who is God. Friends of God! Named in this way, the disciples were not only given a new name, they were also called to a radical new way of being and seeing the world, within which friendship with God, and by implication with one another, became the primary relational currency that was to be a hallmark of God's redemptive love for the world.

It is true that renaming also had the effect of bringing into existence new enemies, people for whom the reign of God and the friendships of Jesus offered a serious threat. When Jesus was named the son of God, the trajectory of his life shifted as this 'new' name drew to it new enemies. Words create worlds. These worlds can be beautiful and filled with peace and hospitable love, or they can be ugly and subsumed by gracelessness.

Giving people back their names

We have seen that mental illness diagnoses are sticky labels that don't just name what we have, but name what we *are*. If you have the virus that causes influenza you are unlikely to be called 'the flu'! But if you are diagnosed with a serious mental illness, you actually *become* that illness; you become 'a schizophrenic', 'a neurotic', 'a depressive', 'bipolar', or whatever names people choose to call you. Mental illness diagnoses are 'I am' labels. If such diagnostic labels were considered to be beautiful things within society this process of naming people as diseases would not make much difference. However, the public image of mental illness is often not a positive one. When you are named as having a mental illness, in a sense you cease simply to be John, Jane or Margaret; no longer can you just be seen to be doing something for its own sake. Now, everything you do and think, all of the ways you act and behave, will be read through your new name.

John attended a conference recently on the role of spirituality in health care. The topic was quite controversial and brought together a theologian and a sociologist to debate the issues. Part way through the sociologist's presentation, he was interrupted by a woman in the audience who was not at all happy with his assertion that religion was dead and that secularism was the way forward. It was an unusual interruption in that normally such conversations go on after a presenter has finished speaking. After much heated argument she sat down. Her points were excellent, even if the space and time she used to make them was a bit odd. After the presentation, the general conversation was around the woman's interjection, with people seeming to assume she was 'obviously' mentally ill. One person even suggested that she had early stage dementia. It turned out that she was a very famous professor of theology who, while somewhat eccentric at times, was a quite brilliant thinker. What was fascinating and quite depressing was the way in which the audience used the label of 'mentally ill' to explain the strangeness of the experience and, importantly, to discount the perspective of the person they had chosen to name as somehow 'mad' (read: 'not like us'). In reality she was a professor; the audience renamed her as 'mad' and in so doing took away her voice.

Stigma occurs when we name things wrongly. The world of stigma is ugly. It destroys and caricatures people and leaves them lonely, isolated and lost. This is why the apparently small gesture of giving someone back their name is profoundly powerful. It is a way of making people who have been deemed to be ugly beautiful again. To name things properly is to act humanly and to bring 'non-persons' back into the community of humanness. The task of the church as it meets with people experiencing mental illness is to model Jesus' renaming of the disciples: 'I no longer call you mentally ill, a schizophrenic, bipolar or any other destructive name. Now I call you friends. John, Jean, Fritz, Mary, Bindhu, Salma, Lee – I want you to be my friends and I hope that you might consider allowing me to become yours.'

When the world backs away and refuses to name people properly, the church must join in with Jesus' words, 'I call you friends.' When people are excluded from communities by the fear of difference, pushed out into the darkness of loneliness, exclusion and isolation, their identities hidden behind names that terrify the world and themselves, the church is called to give people back their names, to whisper or shout, 'I call you friends. I know that you are loved and I want you, not others, to tell me your name.' It is in small things such as this that the face of Jesus is revealed to the world.

CHAPTER 5

From inclusion to belonging

If we practise relating in such ways, things will begin to change. As we name people properly, so we will learn what it means to belong. There is much talk today about the importance of including people with mental illness within society. Once upon a time this movement was named 'community care'. However, it has become quite obvious that there is no such thing as community understood as a coherent loving place where those who are perceived to be different can find a place of love, meeting and embrace. When governments talk about community care they really mean life outside of the institution. Sadly life outside of the institution for those who are perceived as different can be a cold and dark place filled with name calling and the imposition of false identities. The idea of inclusion and the motif of community care require a different form of embodiment. The friendship that is given to us in Jesus calls us to move beyond mere inclusion towards belonging. To belong you need to be missed. To belong others need to long for you like the Prodigal Son's father as he anxiously surveys the horizon, searching eagerly for signs of his son. The friendship that is given to us in Jesus calls us. To belong we need to feel that we matter. Belonging is the true place of meeting. Only when we can come to realise that the church cannot be the church without each member of the body feeling that they belong can we truly be the church. Belonging is the enemy of stigma. Belonging destroys loneliness and fear. Belonging is the heart of the gospel and the true basis for tender meeting. Belonging urges us to alter our hearts and change our minds in ways that enable the creation of new spaces of relating; places where all of us are missed when we are not there. When we offer Christ-shaped friendships within which we truly meet, listen and try to understand, we help to tear apart the bonds of loneliness, exclusion and isolation and open up places of belonging wherein people can reclaim and be proud of their names.

Conclusion: the power of small things

In the face of the therapeutic and pharmacological advancement of mental health provision, engaging in the kinds of small things that we have highlighted in these chapters can appear to be frivolous and perhaps even foolish. However, the calling of the church is not to be clever, but to be wise and faithful to the small things that God calls it to do. Such small things have great power. The task of the church is not world transformation but signalling the Kingdom through small gestures. When we recognise and practise such a calling, it very soon becomes clear that the 'small' things of this world are in fact the very places where the Kingdom of God is encountered most clearly, most transformatively and most gently. Being faithful to the small things of the Kingdom undoes the bonds of violence and oppression and lays the foundations for hope. The church is called to be a community of disciples who love one another with the passion of Jesus, and in their passionate love *for* the world reveal *to* the world that it is loved. To love with the passion of Jesus is to live the life of the church. To offer and receive friendship with people experiencing mental illness is to walk with Jesus, to be a faithful disciple.

PART 3

Resources

This resource section will help your church consider how some of the issues raised in the book can be taken further. Here you find practical suggestions as well as details about key organisations and suggested further reading

Suggestions for further reflection within your church

- Are there ways in which in your church, the story of those with mental health issues can be appropriately heard?
- Having read the stories in this book what can your church learn about helping people with mental health issues to belong?
- If 1 in 4 people will experience mental illness in their lifetime, what does this mean for your church and community, and how do you think you should respond as a church?
- Consider marking World Mental Health Day (10 October) in the church calendar on the nearest Sunday. There are resources available at www.mentalhealth.org.uk.
- Look around for professionals or people in the voluntary sector (e.g. MIND) within your local community who could offer support and training for your church in areas of mental health.
- Consider having mental health resources in your church premises and on your church website.

Organisations you may find helpful

(We are grateful to Triangulate for this information.)

- **Centre for Mental Health**
  www.centreformentalhealth.org.uk
  The Centre for Mental Health is an independent charity working to improve the quality of life of people with mental health problems. They work to influence policy and improve practice in mental health and related services with a focus on employment and on criminal justice.

- **Mental Health First Aid**
  www.mhfaengland.org
  Mental Health First Aid (MHFA) is the help given to someone experiencing a mental health problem before professional help is obtained.

- **Mental Health Foundation**
  www.mentalhealth.org.uk
  The website of the Mental Health Foundation outlines the charity's work in research, policy, service development and service-user involvement. The site offers information and publications to download on research, good practice in services and on mental health problems and key issues.

- **Mind**
  www.mind.org.uk
  Mind has been speaking out for better mental health for 60 years and is now the leading mental health charity in England and Wales.

- **NHS**
  www.nhs.uk
  Search 'mental health' for information, advice and support.

- **Rethink**
  www.rethink.org
  Rethink encourages working together to help everyone affected by severe mental illness recover a better quality of life.

- **Samaritans**
  www.samaritans.org/
  Samaritans provides confidential non-judgemental emotional support, 24 hours a day for people who are experiencing feelings of distress or despair, including those which could lead to suicide. Consider having their information readily available within your church website and publicity.

- **Shaw Trust**
  www.tacklementalhealth.org.uk
  Shaw Trust 'Tackle Mental Health' – your

one-stop shop packed full of information and easy-to-use solutions to help you support staff who are dealing with mental health issues.

- **Time to Change**
  www.time-to-change.org.uk
  England's most ambitious programme to end discrimination faced by people who experience mental health problems. In their site, search 'faith' to find more resources.

- **Triangulate**
  www.triangulate.org.uk
  Triangulate aims to change attitudes and behaviours towards mental illness and to promote positive mental health practices in the workplace.

Worship resources

There are good resources available for including mental health issues in worship.

- The **Mental Health Matters** website (www.mentalhealthmatters-cofe.org) has a helpful worship resource section. Here you will find hymns, songs, biblical readings on mental health, and resources for Mental Health Day, sermon illustrations and talks.

- The **Methodist Church** (UK) has information and resources available. www.methodist.org.uk/ministers-and-office-holders/pastoral-care/mental-health.

- In the USA the **United Methodist Church** has resources available from www.mentalhealthministries.net, including 'Blue Christmas'. This is worship material for churches to use at Christmas, which can be a particularly difficult time.

Further reading

Isabel Clarke, *Madness, Mystery and the Survival of God*, Winchester: O Books, 2008.

Isabel Clarke, *Psychosis and Spirituality: Consolidating the new paradigm*, Oxford: Wiley-Blackwell, 2010.

John Gale, Michael Robson and Georgia Rapsomatioti (eds), *Insanity and Divinity: Studies in psychosis and spirituality*, London: Taylor & Francis, 2013.

Peter Gilbert (ed.), *Spirituality, Values and Mental Health: Jewels for the journey*, London: Jessica Kingsley. 1997.

Peter Gilbert (ed.), *Spirituality and Mental Health: A handbook for service users, carers and staff wishing to bring a spiritual dimension to mental health services*, London: Pavilion, 2011.

Kathryn Greene-McCreight, *Darkness Is My Only Companion: A Christian response to mental illness*, Grand Rapids, MI: Brazos Press, 2006.

Eva McIntyre, *A Quiet Mind: Uniting body, mind and emotions in Christian spirituality*, London: Circle Books, 2011.

Gemma Poncia, *Reflections of a Voice Hearer*, Create Space Independent Publishing Platform, 2013.

John Swinton, *Resurrecting the Person: Friendship and the Care of People with Severe Mental Health Problems*, Nashville, Abingdon Press, 2000.

John Swinton, *Spirituality in Mental Health Care: Rediscovering a 'forgotten' dimension*, London: Jessica Kingsley, 2001.

Jennifer Tann (ed.), *Soul Pain: Priests reflect on personal experiences of serious and terminal illness*, Norwich: Canterbury Press, 2013.

Jean Vanier, *Becoming Human*, London: Darton, Longman & Todd, 1999.

Index

111